The Marketing Toolbox

101 Online Marketing Tools & Resources to Boost Your Business

by Mohit Tater

Your Free Bonus!

As a small token of thanks for buying this book, I'd like to offer you a free bonus gift exclusive to my readers.

This short report is called *15 Best Productivity Tools for Entrepreneurs* and contains a list of all the productivity tools that I personally use. These tools have helped me save enormous time and money in the long run and I am sure they will help you too.

You can sign up for my **New releases** mailing list and get your **FREE** copy of *15 Best Productivity Tools for Entrepreneurs here:*

http://www.entrepreneurshiplife.com/bookbonus

Copyright © 2014 by BookStage

This book is licensed for your personal enjoyment only. This book may not be re-sold or given away to other people. If you would like to share this book with another person, please purchase an additional copy for each recipient. If you're reading this book and did not purchase it, or it was not purchased for your use only, then please purchase your own copy. Thank you for respecting the hard work of this author.

All Rights Reserved. No part of this book may be reproduced in any form or by any electronic or mechanical means including information storage and retrieval systems without permission in writing from the publisher, except by a reviewer who may quote brief passages in a review.

EntrepreneurshipLife.com

For queries, please contact the author by email at mohit@entrepreneurshiplife.com

Table of Contents

Your Free Bonus! 2
Introduction 5
Chapter 1 - Email Marketing 6
Chapter 2 - Social Media Marketing 9
Chapter 3 - CRM 14
Chapter 4 - Analytics 17
Chapter 5 - SEO 20
Chapter 6 – Landing Pages 23
Chapter 7 - HelpDesk 25
Chapter 8 - Communication 28
Chapter 9 – Survey and Market Research 33
Chapter 10 – Pay-Per-Click (PPC) Advertising 36
Chapter 11 – Retargeting Tools 40
Chapter 12 – Customer Interaction & Feedback 43
Chapter 13 – Top Marketing Blogs 46
Acknowledgements 54
About the Author 55
Thank You 57
Can You Help? 58

Introduction

I want to thank you and congratulate you for purchasing my book, "The Marketing Toolbox."

This book contains proven tools and resources to help build a strong online marketing strategy for startups and budding entrepreneurs or anyone who runs a business.

For any business idea to succeed, it needs marketing, period. Sometimes your business might, by all appearances, have everything set in place, but there's something that is keeping it from reaching that next level. This is because at one point or another, your marketing strategy was either incomplete or implemented incorrectly.

What this book aims to provide is the perfect combination of marketing tools to guarantee measurable results for your business or startup. From email marketing to search engine optimization. From customer relationship management solutions to communication tools, this book is your ultimate guide to success. Since I know the majority of you reading this are budding entrepreneurs, I've insured the tools I've listed in each category are both affordable and economical.

Thank you again for downloading this book, I hope you enjoy it!

Chapter 1 - Email Marketing

1.1 MailChimp

Over the years email has lost its shine as the primary mode of communication, but one little chimp continues to make it fun, useful and a great marketing medium for small and medium scale businesses. What MailChimp does is both simple and efficient. MailChimp provides users with the ability to design, send and track email newsletters (across platforms) to a large client base.

USP - What sets this post-monkey apart is its facility to bridge social media networking with email marketing.

Pricing – A wide range of pricing options are available for all kinds of businesses. Its free service provides a limit of 2000 subscribers whereas the $475/month plan allows for 100,000 subscribers and even more. However, the free service does not provide the auto responder service, which is a big miss.

Website - mailchimp.com
Founder – Ben Chestnut

1.2 AWeber

AWeber helps you with automated newsletters and email follow-up service. This ensures brand recall and customer retention. Startups and entrepreneurs in their early stages may not have the time to handle and keep track of all online marketing platforms such as blogs, social media networks and emails. This is where AWeber comes into play.

USP – Automatically generates your latest newsletter with your RSS blog feed and sends it to all of your subscribers.

Pricing – There is no free trial. The first month costs $1. The following months increase to $19 per month, for a subscriber base of up to 500. 25,000 subscribers is around $130/month.

Website – aweber.com
Founder – Tom Kulzer

1.3 GetResponse

Attractive, pretty marketing services can end up being a shot in in the dark in terms of reaching the right target groups. Your startup needs to hit the ground running in as little time possible. GetResponse performs wonderfully as a research-oriented email marketing service with optimized campaigns that let you identify and focus more effort and time on things that matter.

Unlike many other services, GetResponse cannot send emails automatically to subscribers based on the links they click in your emails, but can follow up with auto responders.

USP – Tracking features are very useful, providing data on how many people opened the newsletter, at what time, how many unsubscribed and details regarding invalid emails.
Pricing – From $15/month for 1000 subscribers to $450/month for 100,000.
Website – getresponse.com
Founder – Simon Grabowski

1.4 Mad Mimi

More than 30 color themes, 39 social networking buttons and around 20 add-ons make this email marketing service one of the most delightful to use. Start creating, sharing and tracking your emails with easy-to-use design themes that don't require any design wizardry.

Mad Mimi lets you set up RSS-to-email, Google Analytics tags in emails, connect with SurveyMonkey and add an app to your Chrome browser that displays live reports of subscribers, using the social networking buttons embedded in the emails. Mad Mimi also provides an undo option to restore your deleted campaigns.

USP – Mad Mimi makes creating and sending out email newsletters easy and fun; with its founders and design team

keeping things so simple that even for your grandmother could become an online entrepreneur.
Pricing – Mad Mimi offers users a free option in which 12,500 emails can be sent per month, but offers no customer support. Individuals can opt for the basic $10/month plan that allows users to send unlimited emails to 500 subscribers/contacts.
Website – madmimi.com
Founder – Gary Levitt

1.5 Constant Contact
Email marketing is no longer just about emails, but also includes the integration of online communication platforms and social marketing mediums. Constant Contact is an email marketing service with an easy and friendly user interface. Creating an email newsletter is as easy as picking the right template, then dragging and dropping items. The newsletters can feature embedded videos, images and surveys, which provides a great interactive tool for your customer base.

USP – More than 400 templates are available with the option to insert HTML codes.
Pricing – Up to 500 contacts can be handled with the Basic $20/month package. The premium Ultimate option, with its personal advisor feature, costs $395/month for up to 10,000 contacts.
Website – constantcontact.com
Founder – Gail Goodman

Chapter 2 - Social Media Marketing

1.1 Buffer
In a world of multiple social media services, one tool to manage them all is a much-needed time-saver. Buffer is a one-stop solution to managing your social media accounts by providing automated tweets and status updates. With its smart scheduling features, users can easily plan an update schedule and customize updates individually for each social profile. One of the best things about Buffer is its ability to determine the optimal hour, based on web traffic, to automatically publish tweets and updates, so as to ensure maximum retweets and interaction with the public.

USP – Automated tweets and status updates for social media, with browser extensions for Chrome, Safari and Firefox.
Pricing – A free account is offered, but is limited to only one profile/page on Twitter, Facebook & LinkedIn and only 10 updates at a time using the scheduler. Paying $10 a month provides 12 social profiles, up to 200 posts in the scheduling queue and 2 team members.
Website – bufferapp.com
Founder – Joel Gascoigne

1.2 Hootsuite
This handy web-based application gathers all of your social media profiles into one single dashboard. Quickly viewing and updating all of your account feeds becomes a simple task. The dashboard can compile profiles from Facebook, Twitter, LinkedIn, Ping.fm, WordPress, MySpace, Foursquare and Google+, Vimeo and Wordpress. Users can write, update, schedule and also track tweets and status updates through its simplified interface.

USP – Ease of viewing and updating multiple social media profiles on one screen while using team members or authorized admins.

Pricing – The free version works permanently and is suited to small business owners and individuals, with a limit of managing three social media accounts. The Pro version starts at $9.99/month and tracks 50 social profiles, one team member and offers enhanced analytics report.

Website – hootsuite.com/
Founder – Ryan Holmes

1.3 Ning

The new Ning 3.0 is a major update to its previously ailing social media management software. Ning is an online social community-building platform that allows creators to add members, friends, photos, blogs and profile pages to the community and integrate it with Facebook, Twitter and other popular social media websites. Scope for engaging followers is

tremendous, with the ability to create multiple forums and blogs. Its new responsive design uses HTML5 and works seamlessly on all devices.

USP – World's largest online social community building platform, with social media integration and scope for multiple forums and blog creation.

Pricing – Started as a free-to-use service, Ning 3.0 has become paid with its Basic plan of $25, providing a maximum of 1,000 members and 2 admins. The best option for a startup is the Performance plan at $49 per month which allows up to 10,000 members and 5 admins.

Website – ning.com
Founder – Gina Bianchini, Marc Andreessen

1.4 OnlyWire

Automated social bookmarking. This, in a nutshell, defines OnlyWire. Managing 100 social networking and bookmarking sites can be an overwhelming task. But with OnlyWire, all you do is create your social network and bookmarking profiles and link them with OnlyWire. The next task is simple - sit back, relax, watch and track.

The reporting and analytics tool with this software provides some great statistics about your social media performance and helps measure your return on investment. You can even create teams and assign tasks using the Enterprise edition.

USP – Hourly check-up for new content on your linked WordPress site and RSS feed and automated posting of content.

Pricing – Pro version starts from $5/month and fits the bill for individual bloggers. But for serious startups looking to brand their posts and get detailed analytics and multiple user functions, the Enterprise version starting from $99 makes more sense.

Website – onlywire.com
Founder – Ryan Rouland

1.5 Mention

As a budding business enterprise or as a hopeful startup, wouldn't you want to know how many people have mentioned your brand? And where they are located? This is what Mention provides. It monitors the web and alerts you whenever somebody has made a mention of your company's name, brand or important keywords.

This might sound like an enormously difficult task, but the software does all of the work for you, with a very user-friendly interface. Stay in the loop at all times, across all of your devices, and make sure you respond to any complaints before they escalate into a social media nightmare. Also (this is a secret), you can track your competitors too, using their brands as keywords.

USP – Searches the web for any mention of your brand's name. Ensures better results than Google Alerts.

Pricing – The cost free plan is brilliant to start off with, but its 250 mentions/month limit can become useless when your brand starts growing. The most effective is its Growth plan at $125 per month that tracks up to 10,000 mentions per month.
Website – mention.com
Founder – Edouard de La Jonquière

1.6 SlideShare
With an estimated 600 million monthly site visitors and 130 million page views, this is a presentation party you don't want to miss. SlideShare is among the top 200 most visited sites in the world, and for good reason. SlideShare provides a free-to-use platform for companies and individuals to share their presentations in the form of PPT, PDF, videos and webinars. SlideShare's functionality provides publicity for your brand through presentations & videos, great research materials on different industry specific topics and the ability to share slides between team members.

USP – Largest slideshow sharing community in the world. Users can upload presentations on their brand/industry in any format.
Pricing – Free
Website – slideshare.net
Founder – Rashmi Sinha, Jonathan Boutelle

1.7 Scoop.it
Scoop adds a new phrase to your vocabulary – social media curation. This is not simply a matter of compiling random articles using keywords, but sourcing quality content from the web that will result in increased traffic to your website or social media networks.

Even using its automated curation mode, Scoop understands the importance of manual intervention in the form of quality topic selection. And this makes a world of difference. Instead of blindly copying entire articles, use Scoop to add your own images and teaser content when curating your Scoop page. This assists your brand by giving it a unique edge and, eventually, increasing traffic to your site.

USP – Acts as a museum of online content. Simply chose the topics that matter to your brand. Scoop is the online editor you can't afford not to hire.
Pricing – The free-to-use service is great, but comes with its limitations, offering no scope for teams or the ability to assign tasks. The Professional plan, which includes several more features, is priced at $12.99/month and is suitable for bloggers.
Website – scoop.it
Founder – Guillaume Decugis, Marc Rougier

1.8 CrowdBooster

This is the age of interaction and integration. And CrowdBooster is an online tool perfect for proving both of these essential marketing traits. CrowdBooster measures and optimizes social media marketing. It's tracking is limited to Twitter and Facebook, but you can save time and streamline activities using its auto-post function. Track new fans and followers and learn how to improve your social media presence using its stats on how many times your content has been shared or retweeted. Another great feature is the ability to track and interact with your most engaged fans.

USP – Targeted recommendations help users have a more focused marketing plan, suggesting whom your brand should target on Twitter and Facebook.
Pricing – The Bronze version is good for startups and individuals at $9/month. But it sets a limit of one user and one page/account for Facebook and Twitter. The recommended version is Silver at $49/month, with which up to 8 users can manage up to 10 social media accounts. This also features priority email support.
Website – crowdbooster.com
Founder – Rickey Yean, Mark Linsey

Chapter 3 - CRM

3.1 Hubspot

HubSpot successfully presents the growing importance of inbound marketing, the theory that it is better to be found by customers rather than hunting them down yourself. HubSpot integrates well with third party CRM and API services, such as SalesForce and Zapier. The platform includes an effective CMS that allows for easy website building. Users can nurture and track leads, and enhance results through SEO tools. Improved customer interaction through social media, emails, keyword research and offers are guaranteed.

USP – Successful and proven concept of inbound marketing; easy-to-use integrated set of applications to generate more traffic, sales and leads.
Pricing – Entry level plan starts at $200/month for 100 contacts. For smart content, automated marketing and CRM integration, you should opt for the Pro plan at $800/month.
Website – hubspot.com
Founder – Brian Halligan, Dharmesh Shah

3.2 SalesForce

This is a cloud-based CRM software that has set the standard in terms of clean user interface and easy to navigate design. SalesForce uses smart applications that create a satisfactory customer experience and in turn ensures the acquisition of new customers. Apart from sales and CRM, this online platform also combines service and marketing, providing users tools that can collect customer support requests, assign tasks to teams, solve customer issues, direct customers to online solutions and focus on areas where sales/service can be improved.

USP – Clean and easy to navigate design that combines sales & marketing, contact management, leads under one roof.

Pricing – Packages start from $5/month per user, and run all the way up to $300/month per user. The most popular option is the Enterprise version, which provides customized CRM for your business in entirety.
Website – salesforce.com
Founder – Mark Benioff, Parker Harris

3.3 Ontraport
An integrated platform with an effective CRM, WordPress hosting and several other necessary features for a startup. The CRM engine works wonders, providing a panoramic view of your customers. Users can collect individualized data for each client

and store it in one clean, well-designed interface. The automated task management feature acts like the personal assistant/customer service executive of your dreams.. Target leads with the flexible lead scoring feature.

USP – Reliable, flexible and easy to use with a powerful CRM.
Pricing – Following a three month trial period, the Pro version is priced at $297/month, offering 25,000 contacts and two users, while the high-end Team version, priced at $597/month allows for 100,000 contacts and 10 users.
Website – ontraport.com
Founder – Landon Ray

3.4 ZohoCRM
Smartly designed online service that allows users to keep track of customer interactions and file them categorically. Since the application is cloud-based, there is no need to worry about physical storage space or limited accessibility. The interface is uncluttered, and convenient tabs provide quick access to important data. Zoho also comes with marketing and sales support, providing users the ability to create marketing campaigns, email newsletters and to track competition.

USP – Simple, user-friendly interface with great tools to improve client relationships.

Pricing – The fine people over at Zoho are very considerate with their free plan for entrepreneurs, which provides a great CRM. The only features not included with the free plan are marketing campaigns and sales forecasting. The best paid option would be the Professional, at just $20/month per user.
Website – zoho.com
Founder – Sridhar Vembu, Tony Thomas

3.5 InfusionSoft

InfusionSoft is designed specifically for budding startups and hopeful entrepreneurs. Its vigorous CRM utility lets you gather hot leads, close important deals and organize sales more effectively. Along with a plethora of functionalities, InfusionSoft also possesses useful online tools for increasing online sales and targeting repeat sales.

USP – Easy and user-friendly, even for those without IT experience. Great customer support.
Pricing – The advanced CRM tools are offered by the Deluxe pricing package (with an option to choose between Sales or E-Commerce) at $299/month, which provides a limit of 5000 contacts, 25,000 emails and four users.
Website – infusionsoft.com
Founder – Clate Mask, Scott Martineau

Chapter 4 - Analytics

4.1 Google Analytics

Considered the most useful and easy-to-use web analytics program, Google Analytics leaves no data unturned. The popular Google service translates your website's traffic into meaningful data, covering traffic sources and measuring conversions and sales. Google Analytics tracks every single visitor to your website, be it from social media networks, search engines, referring sites, pay-per-click networks, emails or even PDF document links.

USP – Let's you measure your ROI and focus on better referral websites to increase traffic.
Pricing – As with other Google services, Analytics is a free to use product. However for businesses requiring more features and support, there is a premium service by request.
Website – google.com/analytics
Founder – Paul Muret, Jack Ancone

4.2 Clicky

An alternative web analytics tool option that provides real-time traffic statistics. The service works best for small businesses and blogs. Clicky has the right tools to dig out those links/content on your website that you tend to overlook, but has the potential to increase traffic.

Using its effective 'heatmap' feature, users can identify what attracts which demographics. It also provides a lot of information on every single visitor on your page. Clicky can track Ajax and flash events; the service is multi-platform, so you can stay connected to your analytics from anywhere.

USP – An analytic alternative to Google Analytics. Real-time heatmaps show you which links are hot and which links are cold,

Pricing – The free plan is useful for small users, offering a limit of 3000 page views per day. To utilize the heatmap feature, one must purchase the Pro Plus plan at $9.99 per month, allowing a total of 30,000 page views per day.
Website – clicky.com
Founder – Noah Merritt

4.3 KISSMetrics

"Google Analytics tells you what's happening. KISSmetrics tells you who is doing it." This is the line that greets people visiting the KISSmetrics website. This is a very useful analytics service for tracking the behavior of your customers. The interface is clean and easy to use. KISSmetrics also makes funnels and conversions with an extremely simple API.

USP – Connects and understands traffic in terms of people, even after several months.
Pricing – There is a free 14 day trial followed with plans starting from $179/month, for a maximum of 500,000 events per month.
Website – kissmetrics.com
Founder – Neil Patel

4.4 CrazyEgg

CrazyEgg is a leading analytics tool that helps users dig deeper in order to understand user interest patterns and details, such as operating systems, search keywords and top referrers. CrazyEgg specializes in the following: Heatmaps, Confetti, Overlay Tools and Scroll Maps. Heatmaps are generated on non-links too, a feature missing in Google Analytics.

USP – Great functionality with an intuitive heat map tool.
Pricing – A 30 day free trial is is offered to give the software a test run. The Basic plan starts at $9/month with a maximum visitor limit of 10,000. The most effective plan for the money is the Plus version at $49/month allowing 100,000 visitors per month.
Website – crazyegg.com
Founder – Neil Patel, Hiten Shah

4.5 Mint

Mint is a self-hosted online app that helps you keep track of and improve your traffic. Because the app is self-hosted, it's super fast and lightweight. With Mint, you can find out who has mentioned your brand/site and the method in which they found your website. Mint also boasts a very clean and easy to understand interface in which uses can scroll through data regarding customer visits, referrers, search engine keywords, popular pages and so on, with great ease on the app's dashboard.

USP – Self-hosted by user, so you own and manage your own data; super fast and doesn't need flash.
Pricing – Pricing is fixed at an affordable $30/site you wish to analyze and track.
Website – haveamint.com
Founder – Shaun Inman

Chapter 5 - SEO

5.1 MOZ

The team at Moz has developed what is probably the best search engine optimization software on the market. It is considered "the gold standard" of SEO tools. Moz works wonders for developing inbound marketing. Moz also comes with a superb programming interface and a helpful online community of marketers. The Moz Pro subscription provides access to some great analytics tools and keyword research tools to study competitors' strategies.

USP – Impressive SEO MozBar toolbar provides capsuled reports and comes with a very efficient, vibrant and supportive online community.
Pricing – Try it out for free for 30 days but following this you will have to spend $99/month for standard edition which is worth every penny.
Website – moz.com
Founder - Gillian Muessig, Rand Fishkin

5.2 Raven Tools

Raven was initially developed for the sole purpose of SEO. But thanks to competition and the yearning to create a unique product, Raven now offers a wide set of tools that include integration with other online services such as MailChimp, Facebook and Twitter. But what Raven is most known for is its SEO features, especially rank checking. Using data sourced from Google Webmaster Tools, users can learn more about their SEO performance. Raven's well-designed dashboard is the place to be for any SEO marketer or budding startup looking to improve their online presence.

USP – All-in-one online marketing dashboard with every SEO tool you'll ever need.
Pricing – Raven Pro starts from $99/month, which allows for 4 users and 20 social monitoring searches. The more expensive

$249/month Agency plan extends this to unlimited users and 50 searches.
Website – raventools.com
Founder – Jon Henshaw

5.3 SEMRush

SEMRush is a service that excels in competitor research and shows organic keywords for every domain. Your site will be better equipped to be discovered organically using the effective keyword-position tracking system of SEMRush. The updated dashboard now offers renewed focus on organic & advertising research along with AdSense, backlinks, keyword search tools and ranks. SEMRush is also an expert in keeping track of rapidly changing technologies, so you don't have to worry about your website being left in the dust with old school SEO tools.

USP – Keyword-position tracking stands out from other software, as does its instant updates that let you be on your toes regarding performance.
Pricing – The most popular plan is the Pro Recurring version at $70/month with a limit of 10,000 results per day and 500 keywords tracking.
Website – semrush.com
Founder – Oleg Shchegolev

5.4 Majestic SEO

Explore domains in great depths, compare 5 domains simultaneously, search a large index for keywords for search scores and let sophisticated bots determine the number of backlinks for any given domain and URL. The software focuses on building links and reputation, apart from traffic analysis and competitive link analysis.

USP – Extremely simple interface for researching data on URLs and powerful in backlink exploration.
Pricing – There is a free service for sites with very limited resources. The best paid package would be the Gold at $150 per month, with a limit of 25 million downloadable backlinks.

Website – majesticseo.com
Founder – Dixon Jones

5.5 WordTracker

This app is well-known for its very strong keyword research tool launched in late 90s. It now features an equally powerful link building toolset. With WordTracker, users don't have to wait long periods to study accumulated data because it is offered in real-time. Users can use the app to help boost their search engine rankings, target new markets and attract relevant traffic to sites. WordTracker's video and text tutorials are of great help too.

USP – Keyword results with no waiting time and a popular SEO blog.
Pricing – The best plan for a startup is the Silver package costing $69/month for a keyword result limit of 5000.
Website – wordtracker.com
Founder – Mike Mindel

5.6 Ahrefs

Ahrefs is a powerful tool for link building strategy. It uses its own bot and index which is updated every 15 minutes. Better still, the updated index is usable within 30 minutes. The tool also houses a massive 50 million keywords from more than 10 different nations. A membership with Ahrefs allows access to their Site Explorer, SERPs Analysis and reports. Users with good SEO knowledge can monitor and analyze backlinks to any given site.

USP – Largest index of live backlinks with updates every 15 minutes.
Pricing – Professional plan starts at $79/month for 5000 backlinks.
Website – ahrefs.com
Founder – Dmitry Gerasimenko

Chapter 6 – Landing Pages

6.1 Unbounce

Completely customizable, attractive landing pages from Unbounce will help support your brand's growing image online. What makes Unbounce really useful is its easy integration with marketing tools you already use, such as MailChimp, Google Analytics, WordPress and more. Leads captured on your landing pages can be directly sent to your marketing tools for further data analysis. You can also easily add live chat and surveys to your page.

USP – Perfect for marketing agencies; adapts to mobile phones and is easy to use.
Pricing – For new businesses and entrepreneurs there is the affordable $49/month with unlimited landing pages and 5000 unique visitors per month.
Website – unbounce.com
Founder – Rick Perreault

6.2 LaunchRock

LaunchRock can craft interactive and engaging launching pages while you and your team work hard in the background to create your fully functional website. A LaunchRock landing page can create interest, build an audience and analyze the data – all before you actually launch your site. You gain the upper hand in understanding the interests and moods of potential customers.

USP – Make your site go viral before it's even launched with some great features.
Pricing – As a crowd-funded platform LaunchRock is a free service.
Website – launchrock.co
Founder – Jameson Detweiler

6.3 LeadPages

An extremely simple tool for building great landing pages. Choosing templates and editing content couldn't be easier. LeadPages landing pages can include webinar and sales promotion pages, subscriptions and lead pages. As an admin, users can sort landing pages by conversion rates, redirect web traffic, create pages in minutes without touching any codes and adapt them to their mobile phone platforms.

USP – Create very fast landing pages from over 70 templates without any coding.
Pricing – Pro package at $67/month features every essential tool.
Website – leadpages.net
Founder – Clay Collins, Simon Payne

6.4 KickOffLabs

KickOffLabs is a landing page builder with features not found in other landing page apps, including a newsletter builder, email builder, advanced analytics and unlimited visitors to your site. Some useful template themes can be found in the basic plan, but for better-designed templates, the price increases. While users can edit basic features of a landing page with a simple customizing tool, you cannot start off with a blank page.

USP – Cool and easy-to-use design with unlimited visitors to your page.
Pricing – The $29/month Starter plan is optimal for startups, but limits custom domains to just one, whereas the $49/month premium plan allows five.
Website – kickofflabs.com
Founder – Josh Ledgard, Scott Watermasyk

Chapter 7 - HelpDesk

7.1 ZenDesk

Lower your costs, raise productivity and achieve customer satisfaction using this virtual cloud-based software that operates like a customer relations executive. In addition to its appealing interface, the app integrates well with your support channels such as emails, social media networks and chats. ZenDesk allows your customers to use any online medium to communicate with your brand while Zen offers complete customer support solutions. Gather data and use them to make customer relationships more strong and efficient.

USP – Inbound ticket requests can be handled through any platform.
Pricing – If you simply want to use the basic features and keep the cost low, there is a $1 plan. But the best option would be the $49 per agent/month, which provides insights, an internal knowledge base and time tracking features.
Website – zendesk.com
Founder – Alexander Aghassipour

7.2 FreshDesk

FreshDesk integrates every interaction you have ever had with every customer into one user-friendly interface, thus helping customer support executives solve pressing issues and address complaints quicker and easier. Customer support issues can be directed to the right team member to significantly save time. Communication to and from customers can occur across every platform.

USP – Great customer support from FreshDesk team and simple but effective functionality.
Pricing – The Sprout plan, allowing up to three agents is free of cost while the effective Estate plan, with enterprise reports and live chat features, costs $40 per agent per month.

Website – freshdesk.com
Founder – Girish Mathrubhootham

7.3 Zoho Support

Address support tickets in a systematic, streamlined manner with greater ease. Provide each of your customers their own personalized ticked review portal. Zoho Support has a very customizable and intuitive solution for strengthening the customer support department of organizations. Cloud Telephony for Zoho Support is an excellent feature for building a fully functional call center right within your browser.

USP – Zoho provides a configurable WYSIWYG customization for end users, with no knowledge in programming required.
Pricing – For startups, all you need to do is enroll and have fun. Free forever plan features unlimited agents, community forums, email inbox etc.
Website – zoho.com
Founder – Sridhar Vembu, Tony Thomas

7.4 Desk.com

When you combine help desk tools, social CRM and customer support, you get Desk.com. With its easy-to-use interface & dashboard, social media integration and fast customer support solutions, Desk can bring all your customer service conversations into one window where service requests are prioritized and handled by your customer support team. Your interactions with customers can be carried across email, phone, chat, Twitter, Facebook and more.

USP – A universal inbox for viewing and responding to customer queries from any platform at any place or time.
Pricing – Standard plan costs $35/month per agent.
Website – desk.com
Founder – Gary Benitt

7.5 Deskero

Deskero takes the basic, good ol' help desk system and transforms it into a much smarter and efficient service. The app helps to reorganize ticketing processes and provides companies with a single point of contact for providing a better experience to customers. Deskero's 'One Click Reply' feature lets users answer tickets immediately and set standard replies so that you can look into more important and difficult requests closely.

USP – Complete social media integration with Twitter, Google+, Facebook, LinkedIn, YouTube and more. Enables greater customer interaction and easier accessibility for your customers.
Pricing – Register for free, without any social media integration functionality. The most economical plan would be the Social package, at $15 per agent per month.
Website – deskero.com
Founder – Fausto Iannuzzi

Chapter 8 - Communication

8.1 Prezi

Prezi is, as PC World put it, 'like PowerPoint on a rollercoaster ride'. Probably one of the most important innovations to presentation creation, Prezi offers an online and offline service that allows users to create presentations that look appealing, dramatic and seamless. The beautiful 3D templates are a treat to watch. Your existing PPTs and PDFs can be imported as slides for a quick presentation in Prezi mode. For startups and entrepreneurs, this fantastic presentation making software is a must have to ensure you no longer bore anyone in the boardroom.

USP – 2D and 3D templates with zoom in/out facility; can create and save presentations online, allowing other team members to edit and communicate in real time.

Pricing – Their free service lets anybody create publically accessible presentations using up to 100MB cloud storage. The Enjoy plan provides 500 MB cloud storage and costs $59/year. You also get to make your presentations private. The Pro plan with 2GB cloud storage costs $159/year and allows users to edit presentations both online and offline.

Website – prezi.com
Founder – Adam Somlai-Fischer, Peter Halacsy

8.2 PiktoChart

This online service allows you create colorful infographics, which you can use as an image in one of your presentations later on. Without any design skill or knowledge, users can make their data look pretty and tactful at the same time. Creating an appealing infographic will take less than an hour with ready-to-use themes and very intuitive editing tools. You can upload your own images or choose from an existing pool of icons and graphics.

USP – Lets users turn boring data and statistics into stunning infographics without any design software knowledge.
Pricing – The free version will suffice for individuals and novices, but has limited themes and does not export infographics in PDF or high-res format. The premium account costs $29 per month and lets users remove the PiktoChart watermark.
Website – piktochart.com
Founder – Ai Ching, Andrea

8.3 GoToWebinar
Host real-time meetings and conferences online across devices. Users can invite 1000+ attendees or more to an online meeting and communicate with them using HD webcam video, screen sharing features and interactive tools. GoToWebinar features a built-in toll-free calling option, OpenVoice Integrate Audio, which helps the attendees who do not own a computer mic enter the meeting with a simple phone call. Basic infographics can be used during the webinar to ask questions or represent data for your attendees.

USP – HD video chatting is possible for every participant, without the need for any additional equipment, using HDFaces feature.
Pricing – After a one-month free trial, the pricing is based on number of attendees. For up to 100 attendees in each webinar, it costs $99/month. The popular plan for larger organizations is $399/month, allowing up to 500 attendees. These plans are based on a limit of one organizer.
Website – gotomeeting.com/online/webinar
Founder – Ed Iacobucci (of parent company Citrix)

8.4 BlueJeans
BlueJeans is a video conferencing service that lets users talk between different software. The app offers a cloud-based tele-conferencing service that allows for webinars across devices with easy content sharing tools. The coolest feature is that not everybody needs to be using the same video conferencing solution. An employee using an enterprise solution, such as

software from Cisco or Polycom, can easily connect to those with the more popular Skype or Google Hangout.

USP – Conferencing made possible across all platforms, such as Skype,
Hangouts, Cisco.
Pricing – Plans start from as low as $10/month per user and increase with every additional user added.
Website – bluejeans.com
Founder – Krish Ramakrishnan and Alagu Periyannan

8.5 Enloop

This is a very compelling service for startups and entrepreneurs looking to build their own business plan, but are not 100% sure of how to go about it. Enloop helps you write a professional sounding business plan. The service will also suggest whether your concept will make for a profitable business, and if not, how to improve it.

USP – Customized business plans, with features to forecast the success of your business.
Pricing – For those with a business concept, the free plan is perfect. But for startups looking to build on their own business plans, the Advanced package at $19.95/month works well, allowing up to five business plans.

Website – enloop.com
Founder – Cynthia McCannon

8.6 Infogram

Illustrate your data, choosing from over 30 types of data charts. Edit content on spreadsheets and download the final image or PDF file to your own system. Infographics are created in four easy steps. Infogram is a web-based data visualization service designed to create visually appealing data which otherwise would have been a boring drab. The tool targets people with standard infographic requirements, but without the required design skills. Perfect for journalists, bloggers, teachers and more.

USP – Interactive infographics in minutes with the ability to import your XLS and CSV files.
Pricing – The Basic plan is free whereas the Pro plan will set you back by $18/month.
Website – infogr.am
Founder – Uldis Leiterts, Raimonds Kaže

8.7 Skype
It seems that everybody online knows about Skype. Video conferencing is offered with small groups, 25 participants or less. The service provides voice calls, instant messaging and video calling options. Users can receive calls to their personal phone numbers phone and make calls to local and international numbers at low cost. There is also the paid Skype Manager service which helps small enterprises with a calling-service management tool.

USP – Easy, free and accessible across devices with group video calling facilities.
Pricing – Free to use.
Website – skype.com
Founder – Janus Friis and Niklas Zennström

8.8 Pidgin
Pidgin provides a single app to chat across several messenger services. It understands that in everyone's contact list, there will be a few important people who just refuse to budge from their archaic messaging service of choice, such as AOL, MySpace, Jabber and the likes. An exclusive feature found in Pidgin is that of customized 'pounces', wherein, users can draft custom responses to notifications from important contacts.

USP – Clean and minimal interface with exclusive 'pounce' feature, which sends customized messages to important contacts upon receiving alerts.
Pricing – Free and open-source.
Website – pidgin.im

Founder – Mark Spencer

8.9 Digsby

Digsby is a modernized messenger app. It understands that social media integration is a key to the success of any web-based solutions these days, and that is what it focuses on. Through Digsby, users can connect with any Instant Messaging service, including Facebook Messenger. Users can add their social network profiles and their email accounts, seamlessly updated with every alert. The video and audio quality is decent, with ability to share videos, presentations and more through the messenger.

USP – Great social integration within the messenger app.
Pricing – Free to use service.
Website – digsby.com
Founder – Steve Shapiro

8.10 Appear.in

This is the future of video conferencing. And the future is now. Meet appear.in – an easy, temporary site that allows up to eight participants in a single video chat. All you need to do is log-in, create a group, and share the link. Thanks to HTML5, there is no sign-up required. You also don't need to install flash or any other plug-ins. The coolest feature of all is that each video chat link is temporary, and no data is stored on their servers. The quality of video and audio is good. As Kate Russell from BBC Click said, "It's so easy it almost hurts".

USP – Privacy of content as traffic is SSL encrypted; no installations, no sign-ups.
Pricing – Free!
Website – appear.in
Founder – Telenor, Norway

Chapter 9 – Survey and Market Research

9.1 Bottlenose

A real-time social network content-searching software that finds, understands, compiles and delivers information from all your social networks into one clean interface. The software supports Facebook, LinkedIn, Google Reader and Twitter, siphoning through all the information you receive, whether it be you were tagged, shared, or just all-around popular. Bottlenose not only arranges information from your networks, but also presents it in an in the form of a video or as a static newspaper.

USP - Analyzes all the content and arranges it under their respective themes/genres, allowing for users to click on their topic of interest and read further.
Pricing – Customized as per your need.
Website – bottlenose.com
Founder – Nova Spivack, Dominiek Ter Heide

9.2 SurveyMonkey

Creating surveys is now performed internationally thanks to the help of a friendly, little monkey. SurveyMonkey, is a survey and research tool that can be essential to small business owners, startups and entrepreneurs. Users can create surveys using templates and choose how the surveys are shared. The little monkey does the rest.

USP – Creating professional questionnaires is easy with SurveyMonkey, which also provides a great analyzing tool for better insights.
Pricing – The Free plan is a good start, providing up to a 100 response/survey and keeps a maximum of 10 questions per survey. The most popular plan is Gold at $150/year, with no limits whatsoever.

Website – surveymonkey.com
Founder - Ryan Finley

9.3 Google Alerts

Don't let the free price tag fool you, this powerful service from Google, which searches the web for keywords, is too often overlooked. Google Alerts is an extremely simple to-use tool that monitors the web for the phrases and words that matter to you and sends you alerts in the form of emails. The web-based tool has multiple uses, one of which is to research topics relevant to your brand. By keying in the right search query, you can get all kind of important information on the industry, job opportunities, competitors, news stories and pretty much anything else that interests you.

USP – Extremely simple to-use. Just a few questions needs to be answered and it will start searching.
Pricing – Free to use.
Website – google.com/alerts
Founder – Google

9.4 BizStats

BizStats provides Business Statistics for anyone interested to know more about a particular industry. It can also provide content and statistics, categorized by the type of business, such as company, proprietorship, corporation etc. Researches are attracted to BizStats based on its ability to provide financial ratios. Learning more about a company's financial statement is a lot of fun for startups.

USP – Calculates financial ratios of business organizations through its no login required simple website interface.
Pricing – Free service with ads on the website.
Website - bizstats.com
Founder – BizMiner, PA

9.5 Google Forms

You could call Google Forms a 'quickie survey.' This tool helps create questionnaires and forms that you can be sent to all of your friends, family and/or customers. The survey creation process is so simple you won't even realize your survey is over when you finish creating is complete by the time you're done generating it. Draft website survey forms, feedback forms, online petitions, contact forms and just about anything you want. Google Forms also comes equipped with simple templates to choose from. And the best part? Google Forms is completely free.

USP – Free-to-use with unlimited number of surveys; share results as a spreadsheet.
Pricing – Free service
Website – google.com/forms/about
Founder – Google

Chapter 10 – Pay-Per-Click (PPC) Advertising

10.1 Google AdWords

AdWords is a crucial part of your brand's online marketing strategy. Startups, at some point or another, will require to spend a bit of their time improving profits through advertising and what better way to do so than with the biggest search engine platform on the planet? AdWords can create very advanced campaigns for you on the web, through both mobile and location bid adjustments. Everything about your ad campaign can be scheduled for launch at a later time, which is a very helpful feature.

USP – Comes with the Keyword Planner, which predicts traffic and number of clicks, providing you with insight on the kind of keywords you should be using.
Pricing – AdWords is free to use initially, and payment is made based on a daily budget that you set, or based on the cost-per-click/cost-per-impression on your ad.
Website – google.com/adwords
Founder – Google

10.2 Bing Ads

This is Microsoft's offering of pay-per-click (PPC) advertising, offering ads featured on both Bing and Yahoo! search engines. Bing uses PPC and click-through-rate (CTR) to determine the frequency of an ad. The Bing Ads Editor is a tool to help users draft advertising campaigns offline with the ability to sync once you're online. Users can target specific demographics and increase the bids once you know you are reaching the intended target group.

USP – Target a given demographic of your choice and increase your bid when one target from your demographic has seen your ad.

Pricing – Similar to Google AdWords, Bing Ads is not paid but is a PPC service.
Website - advertise.bingads.microsoft.com
Founder – Tarek Najm, Microsoft

10.3 Facebook Ads

Almost everybody uses Facebook. So missing out on the opportunity to advertise on the biggest online social media party to ever exist does way more harm than good. Facebook Ads can be designed to either take those who click to either your website or to your Facebook page. Facebook offers some very advanced targeting options.

It is important to note that simply accumulating millions of likes from random sources does not help your cause, nor your budget, as much as targeted advertising. Take the time to add keywords, locations, demographics and so on, while creating an ad designed to give your brand more focus. The wider the focus, the less organic and real likes you receive.

USP – Targeted advertising with the option to lead visitors to your site or FB page.
Pricing – No cost to join, based on impressions, clicks and your daily budget limit.
Website – facebook.com/advertising
Founder - Facebook

10.4 Twitter

Twitter, just like Facebook is a great social platform to advertise on. Something that is so great about Twitter, which Facebook does not offer, is that it can be used for crafting very interesting and intuitive advertising campaigns, from teasers to product launches.

Several digital advertising agencies are going the Twitter route as their choice location to pitch presentations to clients. Twitter has moved away from paid accounts and tweets, which were costly and only affordable for big corporations. Now small timers and newcomers can join in the fun with their self-service platform, with which promoted tweets can be bought for cheap and targeted by geography.

USP – More focused and creative ad campaigns then Facebook. No money needed for organic use of accounts.
Pricing – Set an ad budget, which will be deducted, based on clicks and impressions.
Website – ads.twitter.com
Founder – Twitter

10.5 LinkedIn

LinkedIn lets its users create and display ads on important pages within the LinkedIn website. LinkedIn allows only 25 characters per headline and 75 characters for the ad description, which doesn't seem like much to work with, but can be very effective.

What LinkedIn exclusively provides is a very focused target group, categorized by their job profile, company, designation, age, location and industry. This is brilliant for companies whose product is in a unique niche and, for example, requires only the CFOs of companies to take a look. LinkedIn is not just a B2B spot, as many may assume, but a great opportunity for your business to advertise.

USP – Only social media service to let you target your ads based on jobs, designations, industry and company.
Pricing – Similar to other PPC ad services.
Website – linkedin.com/ads
Founder - LinkedIn

10.6 YouTube

They say a picture can say a thousand words. If that is true, imagine what videos can do. With YouTube video ads, users pay only when someone chooses to watch the ad, which is truly great because you can be assured no money is wasted in the process. YouTube can let you target your customers using age groups, gender, interests and location. Also, your video ad can appear over all devices and platforms. The YouTube analytics tool is very useful during your advertising campaign, as it lets you know what is working and what is not. There is however one catch; you have to make a really good video.

USP – Videos move people, and through YouTube it also shared with a large amount of people.
Pricing – Cost per View (CPV) determines the expenses you have to incur which is based on the budget you set on CPV.
Website – youtube.com/yt/advertise
Founder – YouTube

Chapter 11 – Retargeting Tools

11.1 Adroll

Adroll has been in the retargeting business for more than five years now. With easy-to-read analytics, Adroll makes retargeting potential customers a simple task. The software combines with popular advertising partners, such as Yahoo, Facebook Exchange, Google and Microsoft, making it a potential target for 98% of sites on the Internet.

USP – Retargets site visitors who are potential customers across Facebook, Twitter, mobile.
Pricing – Lowest CPM from $1 - $2.50.
Website – adroll.com
Founder – Aaron Bell

11.2 Chango

This software is not just about customer retargeting, but also search retargeting. What Chango essentially does is it understands the potentiality of customers before they even see your ads. This is achieved by learning customer interests and using their recent searches performed on Google, Yahoo and Bing. Chango earmarks every user who lands on any website connected to the Chango network. It might sound a bit creepy from a normal internet goers point of view, but is perfect bliss for marketers and business startups.

USP – Search retargeting gathers information from more than 8 billion search events.
Pricing – The cost varies as per the CPM
Website – chango.com
Founder – Chris Sukornyk

11.3 Perfect Audience

It is all about the simplicity here. Insert a code in the body section of your website, make a list of the type of visitors that you wish to retarget, design the campaign that will be targeted at the specified group of visitors and voila! The service will help you know which sites are receiving more clicks, the response from customers, and which sites you should remove your advertisement from.

USP – Track potential buyers through emails by knowing who have opened your newsletters and who have not.
Pricing – No initial costs with CPM rates from $0.25 - $2.25
Website – perfectaudience.com
Founder – Brad Flora

11.4 Criteo

Criteo boasts of a $6.5 billion post-click sales for its clients in just one year. This is an incredibly good statistic and provides a sense of trust and surety to startups and business organizations. Criteo offers automatic and real-time audience segmentation with its online self-service platform CPOP. Criteo's personalized retargeting technology is what sets it apart from competition as it supports your website's traffic acquisition strategy and ensures consistent ROI and results.

USP – Excels in real time audience segmentation, meaning your ads can change as per the user and requirement, making it more effective.
Pricing – Follows pay per click model.
Website – criteo.com
Founder – Jean-Baptiste Rudelle

11.5 Retargeter

The name says it all. Retargeter basically retargets everything everywhere. It offers site retargeting, email retargeting, search retargeting, Facebook Exchange, CRM Retargeting and retargeting even for short URL tags. Short URL tags help you post links to your advertisement across social networks. Whenever any user clicks on the ad, he/she will be remembered for targeting advertisement later on. Users can target ads according to demographic, location and income of your customers.

USP – Retargeter gives you full access to their network and inventory, whatever your financial situation.
Pricing – To target up to 30,000 unique visitors, a monthly spend of $1500 is required.
Website – retargeter.com
Founder – Arjun Dev Arora

Chapter 12 – Customer Interaction & Feedback

12.1 Kampyle

Kampyle places customers at the heart of its functionality with its efficient Customer Experience Management (CEM). It includes feedback and lead generation solutions. Kampyle also provides integration with and plug-ins for Google Analytics, Google AdWords, Facebook, Omniture SiteCatalyst, Salesforce.com, ComScore, ClickTale, WordPress, Drupal and Joomla.

USP – Ensures feedback from your customers is only shared with your business and not shared with third-parties.
Pricing – Startups can begin with the Bronze plan at $249/month, with feedback items, forms and users limited to just one.
Website – kampyle.com
Founder – Ariel Finkelstein

12.2 Get Satisfaction

The application features Engagement Widgets that let users build an online customer community and gather feedback. Get Satisfaction is also equipped with Community Health Analytics, which compiles a series of reports that allows you to study community feedback and comments, allowing improvements to the actions your business takes. The software also integrates with social media networks.

USP – Creating and cultivating an online community, keeps you in track with customer feedback and morale.
Pricing – For startups the $1200 per year plan works well, with up to three moderators allowed.
Website – getsatisfaction.com
Founder – Lane Becker, Amy Muller

12.3 Temper.io

Temper understands your customer's temper and predicts their mood swings as well. Once Temper measures how your customers feel, your business can work towards improving relationships with those potentially dissatisfied or angry customers. Once you implement Temper, you are provided a constant gauge on the mood of your customers. Using the Temper Tab you can reach out to customers on any page you want feedback on. The Inline Temper is placed directly on a website, while Email Temper asks for the reader's response in every email you send. Alas! If only there was a real-life Temper to gauge the mood of your girlfriend at any given moment!

USP – Let's you predict a customer's reaction and work towards improving customer relationships that are bordering on anger and dissatisfaction.
Pricing – There is a two month free-trial. The best plan is the Pro plan at $49/month offering 1000 ratings/month.
Website – temper.io
Founder – Josh Pigford

12.4 UserEcho

UserEcho offers social media integration, moderation and voting in its community forums. The best part about the software is that it can compile common suggestions and feedback on your products/services, so you get a more complete view on the problems that persist, and can work towards implementing change. You can directly converse with new site visitors using its Live Chat feature and turn them into customers.

USP – Combines discussions, feedback and suggestions. This makes analyzing problems easier and faster.
Pricing – Pricing is $15/month per agent.
Website – userecho.com
Founder – Sergey Stukov

12.5 OpinionLab

OpinionLab excels in listening to your customers. It offers the best benchmarking available in the industry today with over 1 billion pieces of real customer feedback. Data is provided in real-time, which allows organizations to identify issues before it evolves into a bigger problem. OpinionLab will also assist you in identifying opportunities to increase revenue and retain customers at the point of purchase. The software allows your customers the ability to provide feedback, in their own words, at any point of time while surfing your site.

USP – Pioneers in omnichannel Voice of Customer feedback innovation.
Pricing – Payment, like other software in this category, is based on usage.
Website – opinionlab.com
Founder – Rand Nickerson

Chapter 13 – Top Marketing Blogs

13.1 KISSMetrics
The blog from KISSMetrics will keep you up to date on all the latest and important trends in marketing. The blog lets you stay ahead of the pack with interesting insights and reports on the ever-changing aspects of marketing. Read everything about analytics and conversions here.
blog.kissmetrics.com

13.2 UnBounce
Whether you are from event marketing or content curation, you need a smart plan to develop an attractive launching page. UnBounce is now a pioneer in this field and thus it makes a lot of sense to follow its regular updates regarding landing pages, lead generation, conversion and more.
unbounce.com/blog

13.3 Moz
One of the best blogs on search engine optimization with content covering a wide range of topics from content marketing and responsive design to Google updates and building communities.
moz.com/blog

13.4 CopyBlogger
Content marketing articles at its best. This blog will teach you the shortcuts to blending smart copywriting and boring, technical corporate information. Here is the free classroom on writing online marketing content that you wished you could take in college.
copyblogger.com/blog

13.5 QuickSprout
Neil Patel, founder of KISSMetrics and Crazy Eggs is considered one of the most important online marketers. And when Neil talks online marketing, everybody should surely listen (or read). Neil updates once every two days and covers topics such social media marketing strategies to the best content creation tactics.
quicksprout.com/blog

13.6 Social Triggers

This blog comes with a wide range of ideas on how lure random audience into purchasing your services/products. Apart from that, the topics covered look into conversion of online traffic into potential sales. At times, Derek Halpern also writes some inspirational and motivational articles.
socialtriggers.com

13.7 OkDork
As the author of the blog Noah Kagan says, his blog focuses on startups, marketing, self-exploration and tacos. This is a great blog for entrepreneurs. It even brings out write-ups on the finding inner peace and removing stress to enable a more calmer image.
okdork.com/blog

13.8 Mixergy
A lot of great interviews with young and old entrepreneurs who talk not just on their success, but more importantly on why and how they failed. This is key to building a strong foundation for the business. Also get up and close with proven entrepreneurs.
mixergy.com

13.9 Jeff Bullas
A great guide to digital marketing strategies and new age tips. Jeff Bullas focuses greatly on social media marketing and SEO marketing. Read through some interesting articles on simple content writing techniques and how readers can improve upon their 'online-language.'
jeffbullas.com

13.10 Social Media Examiner
Be the master of all things regarding social media. Online social media is presently the most important marketing medium and this blog gives you interviews, insights and updates from the best in the industry. No wonder that this place has more than 270,000 subscribers.
socialmediaexaminer.com

13.11 Occam's Razor
Kaushik is somewhat a star these days with his massive experience in places like Google, Intuit, DHL and so on. So when a marketing person with such great insights into the technology world shares his knowledge, it becomes a must-follow blog.

kaushik.net/avinash

13.12 Content Marketing Institute
The best place online to hangout for content marketers. The tips and tricks of the trade is what this institution shall teach you through its blog. Read on various methods to plan and process some great online conversations that can increase traffic and result in better brand recall.
contentmarketinginstitute.com/blog

13.13 Search Engine Land
Welcome to the land of search marketing. Search Engine Land features posts by industry experts from all digital marketing disciplines. Read about different tactics and strategies that will help you run a successful marketing campaign.
searchengineland.com

13.14 Social Mouths
This blog will make you rethink your Facebook advertising strategy. From the most engaging Facebook posts to the most shared topics, Social Mouths brings you content that is really effective and interesting.
socialmouths.com/blog

13.15 Buffer Blog
Keep up with the latest activities that take place across the world on social media. Buffer Social Blog gives you great content that tells you all the methods to convert your traffic into potential customers. Also get to know what kind of posts are trending on Twitter, Facebook and LinkedIn.
blog.bufferapp.com

13.16 Marketing Profs
This is a place filled with some of the best marketing professionals sharing some very useful content on a wide variety of aspects concerning the online marketing field. Articles cover email marketing, website traffic conversions and so on.
marketingprofs.com/opinions

13.17 Convince and Convert
The blog is one that boasts its #1 marketing blog tag given by the Content Marketing Institute, but for good reason. Convince and

Convert covers content on social media management and research, content marketing, mobile marketing. Best part is its instant updates on the latest happenings in the digital world and how your business can make use of it.
convinceandconvert.com/blog

13.18 Hubspot Blog
The blog from Hubspot understands that traditional marketing no longer exists on the digital space. And thus the articles here follow Hubspot's primary job which is helping companies to attract visitors, convert leads, and close customers. So if your company is one with such a need then this is a blog to watch out.
blog.hubspot.com

Chapter 14 – Top Marketing Podcasts

14.1 UnPodcast
This podcast's popularity is primarily due to Scott Stratten, considered one of the top social media influences of today with a following of more than 165,000 on Twitter. He believes in viral marketing and feels it is time for companies to enter into a dialogue with their customers. There's good reason why his clients' viral marketing videos have been viewed more than 60 million times.
Website, iTunes

14.2 Entrepreneurs on Fire
Interviews of inspiring businessmen and successful entrepreneurs. Interviews are done by John Lee Dumas and uploaded every day. Entrepreneur On Fire was awarded Best Of iTunes in 2013.
Website, iTunes, Stitcher

14.3 The Foolish Adventure Show
Started by Tim Conley, The Foolish Show is for those hopeful entrepreneurs looking into making it big on the internet. Tim's show carries with it valuable information and online marketing strategies shared by Tim using his 13+ years of online consulting experience.
Website, iTunes, Stitcher

14.4 I Love Marketing
They say, for those who want more business than they can handle, this is the place. The shows discusses at length the several communication and business building options through the internet such as direct mails, lead conversion & generation and email marketing. Monday shows are sometimes more refreshing and motivating than your coffee.
Website, iTunes

14.5 Marketing Smarts
The podcasts are updated weekly and features interviews with some of the most accomplished marketing professionals in the field. All you have to spend is 30 minutes once a week and what you get in return is invaluable insights into the latest changes in internet marketing.
Website, iTunes

14.6 The Beancast
Weekly talks and discussions on trends in marketing and technology that affect your brand. It provides content on how to boost engagement and have an interaction with potential customers. .
Website, Stitcher, iTunes

14.7 SocialPros
Here, we get to meet and learn about people working within social media industry in the present times. Importantly, get some insights into the functioning of social media divisions of giant corporates.
Website, Stitcher, iTunes

14.8 Mad Marketing
The Sales Lion is all about inbound marketing and tips and discussions on how to produce some great marketable content. The blog is led by Marcus Sheridan, a partner at HubSpot and a professional on inbound marketing.
Website, iTunes, Stitcher,

14.9 The Marketing Spot
Host Jay Ehret claims his shows can turn regular business into booming brands and amateur entrepreneurs into professional marketers. This is a place for both small and midsized business to dig into the marketing details of social media, email, SEO, mobile, websites and customer engagement design.
Website, iTunes

14.10 Social Media Examiner Podcast
The world's largest online social media magazine features plenty of content on marketing strategies. And while the website is well known for its daily blog content, it also hosts the popular Social Media Marketing podcast show on iTunes.
Website, iTunes, Stitcher

14.11 Social Media Pubcast
Jon Loomer's shows are different in the sense, it steers away from boredom and monotony. The show is best described on the website in one-line - 'Facebook marketing, blogging, SEO tips, discussed by industry experts over a beer.
Website, iTunes, Stitcher

14.12 Six Pixels of Separation
At Twist Image, the idea of hardcore digital marketing is drilled into the company's vision and thus into each and every employee. The same ideology is shared by Mitch Joel, President, Twist Image who hosts the shows. He speaks very meaningful stuff on digital marketing and media hacking.
Website, iTunes, Stitcher

14.13 Internet Marketing Podcast
As UK's most popular podcast and downloaded by over a million subscribers, Site Visibility lets out the industry secrets of digital and search engine marketing. The podcasts will help your business reach out to new customers and generate increased online leads and sales.
Website, iTunes

14.14 Small Business Big Marketing
This is Australian marketing podcast at its best, mate! It is truly a breath of fresh air when online marketing tips and interviews come from another corner of the world. The shows will not only leave you smarter in digital marketing but also smiling. You can also listen to customer feedback and queries being answered.
Website, iTunes, Stitcher

Wrap Up

There you have it! The top 101 Marketing Tools used by today's top marketers and companies. If used correctly, these tools can add thousands of dollars to your business' bottom line and enable you to run a smarter, faster and ore profitable business than ever before.

I hope this book was able to help you understand the aspects of online marketing one needs to consider before investing money into them. It can be truly overwhelming at times, especially for those new to the world of online marketing. I sincerely hope my book has helped make choosing the right marketing tools for your business a little bit easier.

Did I miss anything?
Do you have a favorite tool or resource that I missed out? Send me an email at mohit@entrepreneurshiplife.com and I'll include it in the next edition.

If you enjoyed this book, please take the time to share your thoughts and post a review on Amazon. It'd be greatly appreciated!

Thank you again for downloading my book and good luck!

Acknowledgements

There were so many people that inspired me to write this book, and there were also so many amazing people that helped refine my ideas and make this book come to life. Thank you for your support and for helping to make this book great!

A big thank you to:

- My wife Sneha, for not thinking I am crazy!
- My parents, for I wouldn't be without them.
- All the founders for creating such awesome tools for us business owners.
- BookStage, for publishing my book

About the Author

With over 5 years of experience in digital marketing and working with entrepreneurs and various startups, Mohit has become an authority figure when it comes to growing a business online. He is passionate about writing and runs a New York based digital marketing agency Mixeron.

A self proclaimed hustler, he is a digital nomad and doesn't have a permanent home (he likes it that way!). He has clients all over the globe who consult with him on starting & running online businesses, raising venture capital, online marketing, growth hacking and more. Though he keeps hopping from one place to another, you can often find him working away on his laptop at one of the many New York coffee shops or reading a book in a Mumbai deli.

Drop by and check out his blog at EntrepreneurshipLife.com.
Or feel free to say hi on Twitter or Facebook.

If you prefer email, you can get hold of him at mohit@entrepreneurshiplife.com, he would be thrilled to hear from you!

Thank You

I'd like to thank you again for purchasing this book.

I know there are a ton of books out there on marketing and still you chose to spend your money on this one.

Hopefully, the knowledge that you gained about the various marketing tools will help you run a smarter and more profitable business.

As a special bonus gift, don't forget to grab your free copy of *15 Best Productivity Tools for Entrepreneurs*:

http://www.entrepreneurshiplife.com/bookbonus

If you have any questions or feedback, feel free to drop an email at mohit@entrepreneurshiplife.com.
Your comments are very valuable as they will help me tailor content to your in my future books.

Thanks so much!

Can You Help?

If you liked the book and it was helpful to you, could you please leave a review on Amazon?

I would be grateful and as an additional bonus, send me an email with the link to your VERIFIED review and you'll **get a 30-minute Skype call with me** – you are free to ask me any questions that you might have about **starting, running or growing your business!**

And don't forget, if you want access to more books like this, sign up for my **New releases** mailing list and get your free copy of 15 *Best Productivity Tools for Entrepreneurs*.

Click here to get it now:
http://www.entrepreneurshiplife.com/bookbonus

www.ingramcontent.com/pod-product-compliance
Lightning Source LLC
Chambersburg PA
CBHW051821170526
45167CB00005B/2100